EYEWITNESS
TUDOR

Tudor nobleman

Triptych of the Royal Arms

The Great Bible of 1539

Pestle and mortar

Mary Queen of
Scots' rosary
and prayer book

Thumbscrew

Roasted peacock

Beheading
sword

King Henry VIII

Queen Elizabeth I

EYEWITNESS
TUDOR

Written by
Simon Adams

Tudor noblewoman

Silk mittens, given by Elizabeth I to one of her maids

DK | Penguin Random House

Consultant Dr Lucy Wooding, King's College, London

Editor Bradley Round
Art editors Joanne Connor, Leah Germann, Joanne Little
Senior editor Carey Scott
Senior art editor Stefan Podhorodecki
Managing editor Andrew Macintyre
Managing art editor Jane Thomas
Production controller Rochelle Talary
Special photography Andy Crawford, Dave King
Picture researcher Jo de Gray
Picture librarians Sarah Mills, Karl Stange
DTP designer Siu Yin Ho
Jacket designer Simon Oon

RELAUNCH EDITION (DK UK)
Editor Ashwin Khurana
Managing editor Gareth Jones
Managing art editor Philip Letsu
Publisher Andrew Macintyre
Producer, pre-production Adam Stoneham
Senior producer Janis Griffith
Jacket editor Maud Whatley
Jacket designer Laura Brim
Jacket development manager Sophia MTT
Publishing director Jonathan Metcalf
Associate publishing director Liz Wheeler
Art director Phil Ormerod

RELAUNCH EDITION (DK INDIA)
Editor Ishani Nandi
Project art editor Deep Shikha Walia
Art editor Amit Varma
DTP designer Pawan Kumar
Senior DTP designer Harish Aggarwal
Managing editor Alka Thakur Hazarika
Managing art editor Romi Chakraborty
CTS manager Balwant Singh
Jacket designers Suhita Dharamjit, Sukriti Sobti
Managing jacket editor Saloni Singh

First published in Great Britain in 2004
This edition first published in Great Britain in 2015 by
Dorling Kindersley Limited, 80 Strand, London WC2R ORL

A CIP catalogue record for this book is
available from the British Library.

ISBN 978-0-2411-8758-6

Colour reproduction by Alta Image Ltd, London, UK
Printed and bound in China

A WORLD OF IDEAS:
SEE ALL THERE IS TO KNOW

Queen Elizabeth I's locket ring

Tudor street trader

Rosary beads with medals

Parsley

Lungwort

The Armada jewel

Contents

The Tudor dynasty 6

The first Tudor 8

Tudor England 10

Food and feasting 12

The court of Henry VIII 14

A harsh life 16

The art of war 18

Henry VIII's wives 20

Conflict with Rome 22

The Reformation 24

Tudor childhood 26

Bloody Mary 28

Elizabeth I 30

Tudor costume 32

A golden age 34

Trade and exploration 36

Queen of Scots 38

The Armada 40

Tudor London 42

Tudor entertainment 44

End of an era 46

Index 48

Tudor
noblewoman

The Tudor dynasty

The Tudor Royal family tree

Tudor rose denotes reign of Tudor monarch

John of Gaunt
Henry Tudor claimed the throne through his mother, a great-granddaughter of the Duke of Lancaster, John of Gaunt, who was a son of King Edward III.

In 1485, a new family, or dynasty, of rulers seized the throne of England. From 1399 to 1455, England had been ruled by the Lancaster family, but then fighting broke out with the York family in the Wars of the Roses. The Tudors inherited the Lancastrian claim when most of the Lancaster family was killed. In 1485, Henry Tudor defeated the Yorkist king Richard III and became King Henry VII. The Tudors ruled till 1603.

Arthur
d. 1502

Henry VIII
1509–1547

Wars of the Roses
The 30-year-long Wars of the Roses between the royal houses of Lancaster and York finally ended when the Lancastrian claimant, Henry Tudor, defeated and killed the Yorkist king, Richard III, at the Battle of Bosworth on 22 August 1485.

Mary 1
1553–1558

Elizabeth 1
1558–1603

Edward VI
1547–1553

Both the Lancastrian and Yorkist armies were supplemented by paid soldiers, or mercenaries

More than 80 nobles lost their lives during the Wars of the Roses

One of the ten battles of the Wars of the Roses

Henry VII
🏵 1485–1509

Margaret

James V of Scotland

Mary Queen of Scots

Mary

Frances

Lady Jane Grey

James 1 (VI of Scotland)
1603–1625

Rose: Red and White, from a 16th-century botanical book

More than 17,000 pieces of stained glass make up the Rose Window

The Rose Window at York Minster

The Tudor rose decorates the window

A new rose
The Wars of the Roses were named after the emblems used by the royal houses of Lancaster and York – a red rose for Lancaster and a white rose for York. After becoming king, Henry Tudor married Elizabeth of York, uniting the two rival houses. Henry combined the white rose of York with the red rose of Lancaster to make a new emblem, the Tudor rose. The great Rose Window in York Minster commemorates this union and the new dynasty.

Cylindrical great tower dominates the castle

Outer defensive walls up to 5 m (16 ft) thick

Henry was born in this tower

Welsh connection
Henry Tudor was born here, at Pembroke Castle, Wales, in 1457. He had only a distant claim to the throne but, increasingly seen as a threat to the throne, he was sent to France for his own safety in 1471. Henry returned to Wales to claim his throne in 1485 and most of his troops at Bosworth were Welsh. It is probable that he had spent only a few weeks in total in England before he became its king.

The first Tudor

Henry VII was a shrewd man who, having seized the throne by force, kept it through the subtle use of royal power and strong government. He built up the nation's finances and trade, and largely kept England out of foreign wars. When he died in 1509, England was the most peaceful and prosperous it had been for half a century.

Henry's queen

Elizabeth of York was the sister of Edward V, who was deposed before he could be crowned and probably murdered in 1483. Her marriage to Henry was both a political match, uniting the rival houses of York and Lancaster, and also a love match. They had eight children.

Elizabeth of York

Royal imposters

During Henry's reign, two men tried to seize power with Yorkist support: Lambert Simnel, who claimed to be a nephew of Edward IV, and Perkin Warbeck (left), who claimed to be a brother of Elizabeth of York. Both were crushed.

Securing peace

Flags like this were used to rally knights and soldiers on the battlefield. To break the power of the English nobles, Henry banned them from raising their own armies. This helped end the recurring civil wars between members of the royal family.

Patron of the arts

A cultured man, Henry encouraged French and Italian scholars and artists to come to England. They brought with them the latest ideas from the new spirit of learning, now known as the Renaissance. The Italian sculptor Pietro Torrigiano made this bust of Henry.

Richmond Palace

Henry had a number of royal palaces, but his favourite was Richmond Palace, built by the River Thames in Surrey. He died here in 1509, as did Elizabeth I almost a century later.

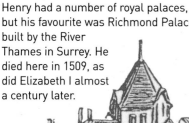

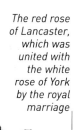

The red rose of Lancaster, which was united with the white rose of York by the royal marriage

Thrifty policies

When Henry became king, England was almost bankrupt after years of civil war. Through careful nurturing of the royal finances, he built up a substantial income and left the crown in surplus at his death. But Henry's policies were unpopular – a year after he died, his two chief tax collectors were put to death.

The Tax Collector by Marinus van Roejmerswaelen

King Henrye the seventh

Encouraging books

Henry and his wife were keen supporters of England's first printer, William Caxton. In 1476, he printed the first edition of Geoffrey Chaucer's poem *The Canterbury Tales*. The stories of pilgrims on their way to Canterbury proved very popular and are still read today.

Caxton's trademark

New worlds discovered

In 1492, Italian navigator Christopher Columbus stumbled upon the islands of the Caribbean while in search of a new westerly sea route to Asia. This spurred Henry to sponsor voyages to North America in 1497 (pp. 36–37).

The *Santa Maria*, Columbus' flagship

Henry's death

Henry died in April 1509 and was buried in Westminster Abbey, as were all Tudor monarchs except Henry VIII. Respected as a king, he was not loved. At his funeral, Bishop John Fisher said, "King Henry, if thou were alive again, many one that is here present now would pretend a full great pity and tenderness upon thee!"

Tudor England

In 1500, England's population was 2.6 million. London was the only big city – most people lived in market towns or rural areas. Tudor society was divided into three main classes: a tiny nobility, a professional and middle class, and a big working class of craftsmen, farm workers, labourers, and servants.

Hard labour

The vast majority of people in Tudor England were agricultural labourers, or husbandmen, on farms owned by wealthy landowners. A few were yeoman farmers, owning a small plot of land, which they worked as a family business.

Wool trade

The export of woollen cloth to Europe was the most valuable overseas trade, rising by more than 60 per cent under Henry VII. Most farmers therefore kept sheep, leading to a shortage of crops.

Hand-spun woollen cloth trousers

Pitchfork

Scythe

Farming the land

Tudor farmers grew wheat, barley, oats, peas, beans, and root crops. They also kept cattle, pigs, and poultry, and worked the land by hand, ploughing the fields with teams of oxen or horses and making their own tools.

Houses had wooden frames filled in with whitewashed brick or thin wood

The farmer's wife

On top of her household chores, a hard-working farmer's wife had to make butter, cheese, and beer, collect eggs and fruit, make clothes for her family, and sell any excess produce.

Meeting and trading

Market towns were the focal point of rural life. They were a meeting place for farmers, traders, and craftworkers selling and exchanging their goods from across the county.

Merry England

Weddings were celebrated with great gusto. Guests contributed food and drink to the feast, and brought their own musical instruments. A good wedding party could continue for days.

Beards became fashionable after the reign of Henry VIII

The middle class

Landowners, merchants, and professionals such as lawyers served in the government, enforced the law as justices of the peace, and sat in parliament. Many lived in small manor houses on their estates, or in town houses.

Glass windows were a recent and very expensive innovation when this house was built in the 1590s

Hardwick Hall, Derbyshire

Noble houses

The nobility lived in ancestral castles or, in later years, country houses with dozens of bedrooms. One such house was Hardwick Hall, built as a display of wealth and hailed as "more glass than wall" because of its huge windows.

A middle-class man could afford small luxuries, such as this fur-panelled overcoat

The nobility

At the start of the Tudor period, the aristocracy consisted of just 38 noble families. Most held great power locally as landowners and employers of rural labour, and lived in considerable luxury.

Food and feasting

Rabbits

The English had a reputation for gluttony among their Continental peers. The rich did enjoy large, expensive meals, but they were as much for show as for consumption. Henry VIII once gave a ten-course banquet for a visiting ambassador that lasted more than seven hours. Even ordinary people ate better than their European cousins.

Tudor kitchen
Grander kitchens had large ovens and adjoining sculleries, cold stores for meat, bakeries, and wine cellars. All kitchens, whatever their size, had an open fire for boiling cauldrons of water, roasting meats and birds on a rotating spit, and cooking stews and other dishes.

Roast peacock
At a Tudor feast, dish after dish had to look spectacular as well as taste delicious. For a "peacock royal", the bird was skinned, stuffed with dried fruits and spices, cooked, and then placed back inside its feathered skin. Tudor cooks also had to stuff swans, bake porpoise pie, and roast blackbirds and larks.

Mint   Sage   Parsley   Thyme   Rosemary

Flavouring
Herbs were widely used to season food and drink, and in medicines. They were collected from the wild or grown in gardens. Imported sugar and spices were pricey.

Easy eating
Even in the noblest house, food was cut up with a knife and then eaten with the fingers. Forks were not introduced until the end of the 16th century.

Classy glasses
Wine glasses were fashionable in the homes of the rich and noble. They were imported from Venice, Italy, and were a costly luxury. Goblets were more commonly made of wood, pewter, or silver and, very rarely, gold.

Crystal wine glass presented to Elizabeth I

Silver spoons
The poor used wooden spoons, but rich people had spoons of pewter or silver. These might be engraved with the family coat of arms, as a way to display their wealth and status in society. Some people carried their own spoons about with them.

Game to eat

Farm workers ate rabbits, pigeons, and other wildfowl they caught in the fields and woods. Fish were caught from lakes and rivers, and capons (hens) and ducks were farmed. The wealthy ate all of these, plus the more expensive meat of geese, swans, boars, and deer, but viewed vegetables as food for the poor.

Pigeons

Goose

English honey

Honey was an affordable alternative to sugar. It was used to baste meats and ferment drinks. Honey can keep for a year or more, and the Tudors suspended fruits in it to preserve them into the winter months.

Fantastic puddings

Sugar was an expensive luxury in Tudor times, so sweet desserts were a sign of wealth. Marzipan, or marchpane – made of ground almonds, sugar, and rose water – was fashioned into castles, animals, or flowers for a banquet. It was coloured using vegetable dyes, such as saffron for yellow and parsley for green.

Marzipan, or marchpane, castle

Decorative rose petals

The stylish spice

Spices from the Americas and eastern Asia were used to season sweet and savoury food, and wine, ale, and other drinks. One of the highest priced and most fashionable spices was nutmeg.

Nutmeg grater and whole nutmeg

Trenchers

At Elizabethan banquets, diners used ornate little trenchers, or square plates, for pastries and other delicacies, then read or sang the verse printed on the back.

The court of Henry VIII

Henry VIII succeeded his father Henry VII in 1509, aged 17. A flamboyant figure, he hoped to make a splash in Europe through both war and diplomacy. He made his court a hub of intellectual and artistic activity, and enjoyed sports, music and dancing, and lavish banquets. Henry's extravagance wasted much of the money his prudent father had saved.

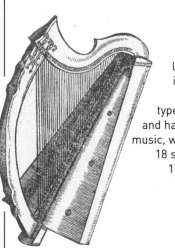

Current affairs
The Dutch scholar Desiderius Erasmus wrote extensively on religious affairs and education, and visited Henry's court.

The Ambassadors, by Hans Holbein, 1533

The Renaissance in England
Henry VIII outshone his father in bringing Renaissance learning to England. This masterpiece by Holbein, his court artist, shows two diplomats with some of the latest scientific instruments.

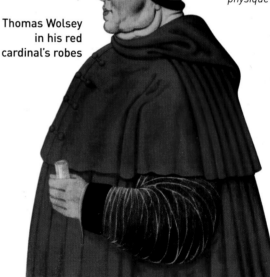

Thomas Wolsey in his red cardinal's robes

Padded shoulders emphasize an imposing physique

Rise and fall of Wolsey
The King's first advisor was Cardinal Wolsey. As Chancellor of England from 1515, he ran the affairs of state for Henry with great skill and made a fortune. He fell out of favour in 1529, but died before he could be tried for treason.

Henry's music
As a youth, Henry learned to play several instruments, including the organ, virginals (a type of harpsichord), lute, and harp. He also composed music, writing church masses, 18 songs and ballads, and 15 instrumental pieces.

A harp of the Tudor period

Pastime with good company, one of many songs composed by Henry

Henry VIII's signature

Fine jewels, a display of wealth

Detail from the Westminster Tournament Roll

A sporting life

Henry loved sport, especially jousting (p. 44). Jousting tournaments were held at court on major holy days and other special occasions. The scene above shows Henry jousting before his first wife Catherine of Aragon, in 1512, to celebrate the birth of his first son. Sadly, the baby died at just three months old.

Hooded falcon

Hunting and hawking

When Henry was not jousting, he hunted stags all summer or hawked with falcons in winter. In 1526, the chronicler Edward Hall wrote that "because all this summer the King took his pastime in hunting, ... nothing happened worthy to be written of."

Ceremonial dagger

Fine gold thread

Field of the Cloth-of-gold

Portrait of Henry VIII by Hans Holbein, 1537

Foreign policy

After invading France in 1513, Henry made peace and married his sister Mary to the French king, Louis XII. More years of war followed until 1520, when Henry and the new king, Francis I, agreed to sign a treaty of friendship. They met at the Field of the Cloth-of-Gold, named after the richly decorated tents erected there. Two years later they were at war again.

Kingly stature

The young king stood 193 cm (6 ft 3 in) tall, with broad shoulders, fair skin, and red hair. He was highly intelligent, wrote books on theology, and revelled in intellectual debate. A lifetime of eating and drinking heavily took its toll, however, and in later years he became so fat that special machines were needed to haul him up stairs or on to his horse.

Henry rides to meet the French king

A harsh life

For most people in Tudor England, life was far from easy. An array of deadly diseases threatened to cut lives short. Medicine was primitive and the average life expectancy was only about 35 years. For those who fell foul of the law, punishment was cruel, and serious crimes often incurred torture and execution.

Brief childhood
Out of every 100 Tudor babies born, only 70 reached their first birthday and only 50 saw the age of five. Typhus, smallpox, and other deadly diseases were a constant threat.

Cauterizing iron

The plague
The boils of plague victims were cauterized, or sterilized, with a red-hot iron. But the plague was untreatable, and could be contained only by isolating the affected and leaving them to die.

Long-nosed mask for a snoop or meddler

Masks of shame
For anti-social behaviour such as gossiping or nosiness, the punishment was usually public humiliation. The offenders were made to walk through the streets wearing comical masks that mocked their crime, and endure ridicule from the townspeople.

Marjoram to ease bruises and swellings

Feverfew for headaches and childbirth

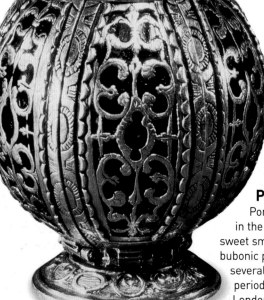

Lemon balm for most ailments and illnesses

Medicinal herbs
A wide range of herbs were used in medicine. Some were fanciful, but many, such as lemon balm, are still used today. Herbalists played a similar role to present-day doctors.

Pomander – container for aromatic herbs

Perfume power
Pomanders were carried in the vain hope that the sweet smell would ward off bubonic plague, which struck several times in the Tudor period. In 1563–64, 17,000 Londoners died – about one-sixth of the city.

Lungwort to treat chest disorders

Tudor whipping flail

Flail to whip beggar

Scavenger's Daughter

Whipped out of town
Tudor governments believed in helping the deserving poor, but able-bodied people who resorted to begging or stealing got a public whipping through the streets.

Torture devices
Prisoners in the Tower of London faced several forms of torture. They might be stretched on a rack or crushed by the Scavenger's Daughter – a metal band wrapped around the victim and tightened by a giant screw, forcing him to crouch with his shoulders close to his knees.

Thumbscrew

Mask for a gossip

Naked sinners guarded by devils

Sentenced to death
Murder, treason, witchcraft, highway robbery, and desertion in war were all punishable by death. High-ranking people were beheaded, but commoners were hanged.

Gruesome warning
The heads of traitors executed in London were placed on sticks on London Bridge as a warning to others. In 1599, a visitor from Switzerland saw more than 30 in place.

Torments of Hell
To most people in Tudor England, Hell was a real and terrifying place. Whether Protestant or Catholic, the Church taught that eternal damnation awaited anyone whose sins outweighed their good deeds.

The art of war

Soldier using early firearm

Tudor England was often threatened with invasion by Scotland, Ireland, France, and the Netherlands, and with internal dissent. National defences were a major preoccupation, and the art of warfare developed considerably. Traditional longbows, lances, and swords gave way to firearms, and forts now had to withstand the new firepower of cannons.

Reinforced breastplate for protection against blade and shot

Plates could be lowered to the allow air in

Hinged plates allow knees to bend

Armour was made from steel

The Battle of Flodden

In 1513, James IV of Scotland invaded England after Henry VIII attacked France, an ally of the Scots. He was killed at Flodden, along with most of the Scottish nobility. In 1542, his son James V invaded Engand. His army was also defeated.

Unlucky *Mary Rose*

The pride of Henry VIII's navy was the *Mary Rose*, built in 1509–10. One of the most advanced ships of its time, it was believed that no town in the world could withstand its firepower of 207 guns. But in 1545, in a sudden gust of wind, the ship capsized and sank, drowning 470 men.

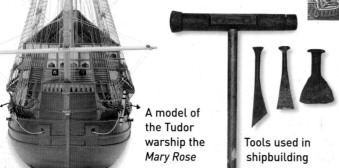

A model of the Tudor warship the *Mary Rose*

Tools used in shipbuilding

Shipbuilding

Henry VIII's demand for a modern, powerful navy led to the world's first dry dock at Deptford, on the River Thames. Hundreds of shipwrights built hulls of oak from the forests surrounding London.

Two bows

Double bowstring

Before the Tudor age, the traditional weapon of the English was the longbow. Its steel-tipped arrows could reach their target from up to 90 m (100 yards) away. By the early 1500s, the crossbow was being used more often. Loaded by a mechanical device, it achieved an even greater range and accuracy.

South coast defences

In the late 1530s, England faced the threat of France and the Holy Roman Empire – made up of the different Germanic territories – acting together to re-impose Catholicism. Henry VIII strengthened England's defences by building five forts on the south coast, including this one at Deal, Kent.

Crossbow

A piercing weapon

As firearms increased in power, hand-held weapons such as pikes and lances became less effective in battle, but swords were still used in close-combat fighting.

Double-edged blade

16th-century sword

Close combat

This armour was made in 1587 at the workshops set up by Henry VIII in Greenwich. Suits of armour were costly and only the nobility could afford them.

They were useful in close-combat fighting as protection against hand-to-hand weapons. By the late Tudor period, the increasing use of firearms led to a decline in full body armour.

Cavalryman with wheel-lock pistol

Arming the troops

During the 1500s, mounted soldiers began to use pistols in place of lances. Wheel-lock pistols worked in all weathers and could be fired with one hand, unlike the earlier matchlocks. The flintlocks of the 1600s would be even more efficient.

Gunpowder

Ornate wheel-lock pistol

Henry's navy

Henry VIII was the first king to keep a permanent navy. Before him, monarchs hired ships from private owners when the need arose. When Henry became king, there were just seven permanent ships in the English navy. By 1545, a fleet of 80 ships was ready to fight the French navy.

Embarkation of Henry VIII on board the *Henry Grâce-à-Dieu* in 1520

Henry VIII's wives

Henry VIII's first marriage was one of political convenience. It lasted 24 years but produced only one child, a girl. Desperate for a male heir, Henry had the marriage cancelled, or annulled, in 1533. Only his sixth and final wife escaped either death or divorce.

The only son

In 1537, Jane Seymour gave birth to a son, Edward, but died only days later. In 1553, Edward too fell ill and died, aged 15 (p. 28).

Lettering decorated with gold leaf — Nativity scene

Anne's prayer book

This Book of Hours, a bound collection of prayers and religious meditations, belonged to Anne Boleyn, and may have given her comfort before her execution.

Another daughter

Anne Boleyn's daughter Elizabeth, the future queen, was born in 1533. She was christened, wearing this robe, at Greenwich Palace on the River Thames.

Catherine of Aragon

Henry's first wife

Catherine of Aragon (1485–1536) was the daughter of the king and queen of Spain. She was originally married to Henry's older brother, Arthur, who died in 1502. She then married Henry, but only one daughter, Mary, survived.

Anne Boleyn

Henry fell in love with Anne Boleyn (c. 1501–36) in 1525. She refused to be just his mistress, and married him in secret in 1532 – before his first marriage was annulled. After her failure to produce a son, Henry lost interest in Anne. In 1536, she was beheaded on charges of adultery.

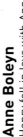

The initial of Anne's surname

Jane Seymour

Just 11 days after Anne Boleyn's execution, Henry married Jane Seymour (c. 1509–37), one of Anne's ladies-in-waiting. Tragically, Jane died soon after a longed-for son was born.

Beheading sword, made by a German craftsman

A sharp, swift instrument

Anne Boleyn and Catherine Howard were both executed for adultery. Given their royal status, they were beheaded with a sword, not the blunt axe used for commoners.

"Even if I were to suffer a thousand deaths, my love for you would not abate one jot."

ANNE BOLEYN TO HENRY VIII

Anne of Cleves

Henry agreed to marry Anne of Cleves (1515–57) after being shown this portrait. She was the daughter of a German prince, and the marriage was meant to deepen England's ties with German states against Catholic powers. Anne did not live up to her portrait – Henry divorced her in 1540, after just six months of marriage.

Catherine Howard

A cousin of Anne Boleyn, Catherine Howard (c. 1525–42) married Henry just days after his divorce from Anne of Cleves. She was 19 and he 49. In 1542, she too was executed for adultery.

Catherine Parr

Henry married his sixth and final wife Catherine Parr (c. 1512–47) in 1543. Learned and sensitive, she proved an ideal stepmother for the three children, and looked after Henry until he died in 1547.

Traitors' Gate, through which boats brought important prisoners

In the tower

The Tower of London was both a royal residence and a prison. Henry's first two wives stayed here before being crowned queen in Westminster Abbey. Anne Boleyn and Catherine Howard were put to death inside its walls.

Conflict with Rome

In 1533, when Henry had his first marriage annulled without papal consent, the Pope excommunicated him (excluded him from the Roman Catholic Church). In 1534, Henry retaliated by getting parliament to pass the Act of Supremacy, which established him as Supreme Head of the Church of England and marked a break with Rome.

The wealth of the Church
The Church and the monastic orders in England owned large estates and had acquired huge wealth. Henry now claimed these for the throne.

Sapphire

Gem-encrusted priest's chain

Nativity scene

Authority of the Pope
Although sovereign (answering to no one but God) in their own land, all Christian monarchs in western Europe accepted the supreme authority of the Pope in Rome.

Luther and his theses
In 1517, German theologian Martin Luther issued a list of 95 arguments, or theses, against corruption in the Catholic Church. A religious revolution, the Reformation, soon swept across Europe.

Luther nails his 95 theses to a church door in Wittenberg, Saxony

Dissolution
By 1535, Henry VIII had taken on the role of Church reformer. By 1540, every monastery, abbey, friary, nunnery, and convent had been charged with corruption and closed, or dissolved. Their lands and other valuable assets were taken over by the King.

The roof was removed for its valuable lead

Fountains Abbey, Yorkshire, dissolved in 1539

The burning of
Anne Askew

Anne Askew

Influenced by the new Protestant ideas of Europe's Reformation, many women became active in religion and politics. Anne Askew left her husband and distributed Protestant pamphlets, including some, unwisely, to Catherine Parr, Henry's last wife. Askew was arrested, tortured on the rack, and then burned at the stake in 1546.

A monk teaching children before the dissolution of the monasteries

Community work

Monks had taught children Latin, theology, and other subjects, and given food and help to the poor and old. Without the monasteries, education suffered and rural poverty now increased.

Coverdale's
Great Bible

Illuminated initial letter (decorated, and with a picture inside it)

Lost skills

The dissolution of the monasteries caused widespread artistic desecration. Many of the precious manuscripts copied and decorated by skilled monks and nuns were either destroyed or sold into private hands.

Doing the King's work

Thomas Cromwell, one of Henry's top advisors, organized the separation of the English Church from Rome. He also arranged the dissolution of the monasteries, boosting the royal purse, and government reform. Blamed for Henry's fourth marriage, he was executed on a trumped-up charge of treason in 1540.

The Bible

All bibles in England were written in Latin. In 1537, Henry VIII furthered his break from Rome by authorizing an English translation. In 1539, a translation by Miles Coverdale was issued and became the authorized edition for use in churches until 1571.

The Reformation

The protectors
Edward VI's Protector was his uncle Edward Seymour, Duke of Somerset (above), followed by John Dudley, Duke of Northumberland, after 1550.

Edward VI was only nine years old when he succeeded his father Henry VIII in 1547, so the government was run by a Protector. Under his guidance, and with the Protestant king's consent, the Archbishop of Canterbury could consolidate the Reformation begun under Henry. The old Catholic Church was swept away and a new Protestant Church set up.

Protestant reformer
The Archbishop of Canterbury, Thomas Cranmer, supported Henry VIII's break with Rome. In 1549, he wrote the first Book of Common Prayer, replacing the Latin prose with English.

Tudor succession
Designed as propaganda, this painting shows the triumph of the Tudor monarchy against the Catholic Church. The ailing Henry VIII passes on the succession to his son Edward, supported by his leading nobles and clerics. At their feet lies the defeated Pope.

Henry VIII

Edward VI

Duke of Somerset, Lord Protector of England

Duke of Northumberland

Thomas Cranmer, Archbishop of Canterbury

St Mary Bethlehem hospital, London, re-established by Edward VI

New hospitals
Before the dissolution of the monasteries, monks and nuns were the main providers of care for the sick. Under Edward VI, hospitals reopened under state, or secular, ownership.

Stripping the churches

During the reign of Edward VI, between 1547 and 1553, almost all medieval English church art, statues and icons, prayer books, hymnals, and other books and manuscripts were destroyed. The Catholic Mass became illegal. Two Acts of Uniformity, in 1549 and 1552, demanded that everyone accept the new Protestant religion.

Rosary with medals of saints

Rosary beads
The rosary is the series of prayers recited by Roman Catholics and counted out on a string of beads. The rosary was now forbidden and the use of rosary beads outlawed.

Jesus on the cross

Rood screens
In Catholic churches an ornate screen with a crucifix, or rood, separated the clergy at the altar from the congregation. Many rood screens were now removed, to bring clergy closer to their flock.

Valuables
In 1550, the clergy was instructed to eliminate all traces of idolatry. Gold and silverware, such as this chalice for communion, was sold or melted down, boosting the royal finances.

Plain whitewashed walls

Heads of saints decorate the chalice

Virgin Mary and baby Jesus

Removing icons
As part of the ban on idolatry, or "idol-worship", statues and icons of the Virgin Mary and the saints were taken away from churches.

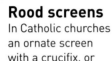

Simple interiors
Every church and cathedral was stripped of Catholic imagery, so worship could focus on God alone. Statues were smashed, altars torn out, chapels destroyed, and beautiful wall paintings whitewashed over.

Tudor childhood

In Tudor times, childhood was often brief. Privileged boys went to school, or were educated by tutors, learning subjects such as Latin, the language of the Church, and law. Only the most highborn girls were educated. From the age of seven, poorer children left home to become apprentices or servants. Girls could be married at 12 and boys at 14.

The Lord's Prayer in Latin

A well-to-do Tudor schoolboy

Hornbook
Children learning to read were given prayers and Bible verses written on a sheet of paper fixed to a piece of wood and covered in transparent horn for protection.

Learning to write
Writing was done with a quill pen, usually made from a goose feather, whose tip was cut at an angle to make the nib, then dipped in ink stored in horn or pottery inkwells. Many of those who learned to read never learned to write.

Horn inkwells

Goose-feather quills

Basic education
Infants received basic learning at "petty" or "dame" schools or at the local church hall. At six or seven, some richer boys went on to grammar schools. Poorer boys started learning a trade.

Pupils line up to recite their Latin grammar, hoping to avoid a thrashing

Keeping order in the classroom
Tudor students were regularly whipped with canes, bundles of birch twigs, or leather straps, as most teachers and educational theorists believed that pain was good for the soul. The scholar Erasmus advocated humane treatment in his book *On The Teaching of Boys*.

A professional training
Guildford's Royal Grammar School was founded by Edward VI, and is still in use today. Tudor grammar schools combined classical subjects such as Latin grammar, logic, and rhetoric with practical skills such as writing and arithmetic.

Names of old students inscribed on beams

THOMAS BAKER. MAIOR 1565.

Higher education

University education was available for bright grammar school boys as young as 14, at either Oxford or Cambridge, the only two universities then in existence. There they could study divinity, civil law, physic (medicine), Hebrew, and Greek.

Christ Church College, Oxford, founded in 1546

Tudor rocking horse

Children are among the workers at this 16th-century printing press

Child labour

At seven to nine, many poorer children, mostly boys, left home to become apprenticed to a craftsman. Tied to the master by a strict oath, and given lodging, food, clothes, and tools, the boy learned the trade by assisting his master.

Tudor toys

The nurseries of richer children were filled with rocking horses, wooden toys and games, dolls, and model ships and castles. Poorer children made their own toys out of scraps of wood lying about the farm or street.

Playtime

No playgrounds were provided for children, so they played out in the street and made up their own games. They enjoyed spinning wooden hoops and playing leapfrog, catch, bowls, and the then extremely violent game of football.

Playing leapfrog

Spinning a hoop

Three Sisters by an unknown 16th-century artist

Children from a wealthy family wore fine jewellery

Tiny adults

Tudor babies were swaddled in layers of tightly wrapped cotton to make their limbs grow straight. Children wore miniature versions of their parents' clothes and learned to behave formally. When their parents entered the room, boys took their caps off and girls had to curtsey.

Bloody Mary

Before Edward VI died, he nominated Lady Jane Grey, the Protestant granddaughter of Henry VIII's sister, as his heir. The country supported Mary, Henry's eldest child, as his legitimate heir. In 1553, she became the first English female monarch in four centuries. She restored Catholicism as the state religion and began a campaign against the enemies of God. The burning of 300 Protestants during her reign gained her the name "Bloody Mary".

Back to Rome
Under Mary, papal supremacy was restored, as were the Mass and Catholic clergy. All the Protestant legislation of the past decades was repealed.

Ornate Catholic cross

A troubled life
A devout Catholic, Mary was personally responsible for much of the religious persecution during her reign. She wanted desperately to have a child to prevent her Protestant sister Elizabeth succeeding to the throne. But she died childless, probably of cancer, aged 42.

Queen for nine days
When Edward died on 6 July 1553, Jane was proclaimed queen. Nine days later, Mary marched on London with her supporters and took her rightful throne. Lady Jane Grey was beheaded in 1554.

The apostle Mark

Burned alive

The Protestant martyr Archbishop Cranmer had arranged Henry VIII's divorce from Mary's mother. In 1556, he was burned at the stake for heresy – having the wrong religious beliefs.

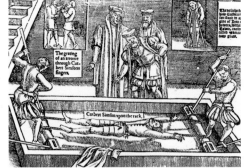

On the rack

After Mary's death, John Foxe compiled a *Book of Martyrs*, with accounts of all who had been burnt or punished for their beliefs. Here, a heretic is tortured on the rack.

Loss of Calais

By Mary's reign, the port of Calais was the last of England's possessions in France. In 1557, England and Spain declared war against France, Spain's main enemy in Europe. When the French took Calais, its loss was a national humiliation, and Mary took it as a personal failure.

Luke, one of the four apostles shown on this cross

Calais with its protecting sea wall

Enamel plaque showing the capture of Calais in 1558

Anti-Catholic satire

This painting shows Stephen Gardiner, Bishop of Winchester and Mary's Lord Chancellor, eating a lamb. It mocks the Catholic Mass, when a wafer is believed to become the body of Christ and is referred to as the lamb of God.

Philip of Spain

When Mary married Philip, heir to the Spanish throne, many people did not want a Catholic foreigner sharing the throne, and saw Spain as an enemy. In 1556, Philip became king of Spain and left, two years before Mary died.

"When I am dead and opened, you shall find 'Calais' lying within my heart."

Attributed to Queen Mary I on the loss of England's only continental possession

29

Suspicious sister

In 1554, Elizabeth was imprisoned by her sister Mary I in the Tower of London on suspicion of treason. Mary believed Elizabeth had been involved in the short-lived Wyatt rebellion against her rule, though no actual evidence of this existed.

Elizabeth I

Elizabeth became queen after the death of her sister Mary I in 1558, but her position was far from secure. Many Catholics did not want her as queen because she had been declared illegitimate as a child. By skilfully instating a benign form of Protestantism, she succeeded in containing the unrest and securing her own position.

Elizabeth in her coronation robes

Royal sceptre, symbol of sovereignty

Ring of affection

Elizabeth's mother Anne Boleyn was executed for adultery when Elizabeth was only three years old. One of the few reminders of her mother was this locket ring.

Anne Boleyn, Elizabeth's dead mother

Elizabeth

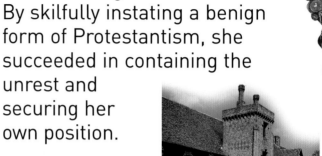

Childhood home

Elizabeth spent much of her childhood at Hatfield House in Hertfordshire, and it was her main home from 1555–58. It was here, while sitting under an oak tree, that she heard the news of her sister's death and that she was to be Queen. Overcome, she knelt and said, quoting Psalm 118, "This is the Lord's doing; it is marvellous in our eyes."

16th-century opharian

Mother-of-pearl locket ring opens to reveal family portraits

12 wire strings

Orpharian player

Inset pearls

Scholar and musician

Like Mary, Elizabeth was a fine linguist, reading Latin and Greek fluently as well as speaking many European languages. She was also an accomplished poet. She enjoyed dancing and hunting, and was a skilled musician. This ornate orpharion was once owned by Elizabeth.

Decorative walnut inlay

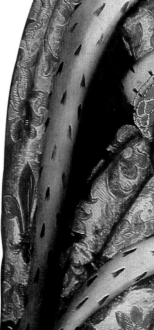

Royal footmen

Elizabeth's coronation procession

The coronation

On 15 January 1559, Elizabeth processed from the Tower of London to the palace of Whitehall. Crowds lined the streets, which were decorated with banners and streamers. The next day, she walked along streets that were covered with blue cloth to be crowned queen in Westminster Abbey.

Character of a queen

Elizabeth had inherited her father's red hair and fair skin, and much of his charisma. Intelligent, shrewd, and tolerant, she could also be impetuous, vain, and sarcastic.

Faithful advisor

William Cecil served Elizabeth loyally for 40 years as Secretary and Lord Treasurer, and worked tirelessly to support her authority.

Orb, a symbol of royal power and justice

A moderate

The man most responsible for England's return to a moderate form of Protestantism was the Archbishop of Canterbury, Matthew Parker. A wise and learned scholar, he also helped to preserve medieval manuscripts.

Royal coat of arms from the Church of St Mary's, Suffolk

Elizabethan religion

When the Protestant religion was reinstated, Elizabeth was made Supreme Governor of the Church and the royal coat of arms was hung on the wall in most churches. Elizabeth was not as zealous in her religion as her Protestant brother and Catholic sister, and held back from a vigorous persecution of religious difference.

Tudor costume

In Tudor times, strict regulations stated what could and could not be worn. These Sumptuary Laws enforced the wearing of English-made cloth in an attempt to bolster the home textile industry. They also upheld distinctions between the social classes by confining the wearing of finer fabrics to the nobility.

French hood, made popular by Anne Boleyn

Gown, worn fashionably over the shoulder

Men were clean-shaven in early Tudor times

Gold, emerald, and diamond hat jewel

Fire jewel
Since the salamander was thought to be able to survive fire, this jewel was worn to suggest strength and vigour.

Early Tudor woman
Well-dressed women at the start of the Tudor period wore heavy, floor-length gowns of velvet or silk. Necklines were often decorated with jewels, and the bodice below had embroidered panels. Hair was swept back and under a hood.

Richly patterned doublet

Close-fitting tights, or hose, attached to the doublet by laces

For men
Men wore a shirt of wool, linen, or silk. Over this they wore a close-fitting jacket, or doublet. A working man wore a woollen jerkin or jacket, while a rich man wore a short-sleeved robe or gown. Wealthy men's clothes were often made from heavy, patterned fabrics.

Cotton underskirt beneath velvet gown

Elizabethan man

After about 1540, men began to wear a padded, round trunk below the waist, breeches down to the knee, and stockings underneath. The doublet was padded both at the shoulders and at the hips. This made a man look broader at the shoulders and narrower at the waist.

Starched linen ruff

Jewelled band to keep hair off face

Ruffs around the wrists match the neck ruff

Cinnabar used for red blusher

Mixing make-up

The bright-red mineral cinnabar was used as a rouge, and tin made the cheeks white. Make-up was prepared by mixing minerals such as talc with fig juice and other liquids and grinding them to a paste in a pestle and mortar.

Talc

Pestle and mortar

Fig

Tin

New cap

In 1571, a new law ordered everybody over six and below a certain rank to wear a woollen cap on Sundays and holidays.

Padded, decorated trunk

Velvet breeches, or canions

Fashion sense

Wide shoes became so fashionable in Tudor times that, under Henry VIII, a law limited their width to 15 cm (6 in).

Elizabethan woman

Wide dresses padded out over frames of wire, cane, or whalebone emphasized narrow waists. Necklines stayed square-cut and low, with a frill collar around the neck, and shoulders were padded and frilled.

Gable hood with padded band decorated with jewels

Fashionable headdress

The gable hood was made popular in England by Henry VIII's first wife, Catherine of Aragon. Made of rich fabric such as velvet or damask, it was worn over a tight-fitting undercap and reached half-way down the back.

Stately gloves

Noble women wore ornate, perfumed gloves. This pair was given to Elizabeth I when she visited the University of Oxford in 1566.

A golden age

Under Elizabeth, England became a major European power, and art and culture flourished. Female leaders were rare, and it was unheard of for one to remain single. Elizabeth would not share the throne, saying that she was "married to England". She kept up this popular image by making skilful speeches and controlling how she was portrayed.

Egg white

Poppy seeds

Presenting a face
As she aged, Elizabeth was careful to appear as young as possible in public. She wore elaborate make-up to cover her smallpox scars. But the lead and mercury base of most cosmetics then used were toxic, and badly damaged the skin.

Elizabeth wore a full wig to conceal her grey hair

Pelican's bloody chest, a symbol of sacrifice

A mother's love
Pelicans were thought to feed their young on their own flesh. Elizabeth wore this brooch as a symbol of her motherly self-sacrifice for her subjects.

Representing the Queen
Hundreds of paintings of Elizabeth were made during her lifetime, but few were done directly from life. One painting served as a template for others, showing her as a symbol of England's power.

Pearls symbolized chastity

Deadly smallpox
In 1562, Elizabeth caught smallpox. This medal commemorates her recovery. Like St Paul when he was bitten by a snake, the Queen was said to be unscathed.

Globe, a symbol of imperial domination

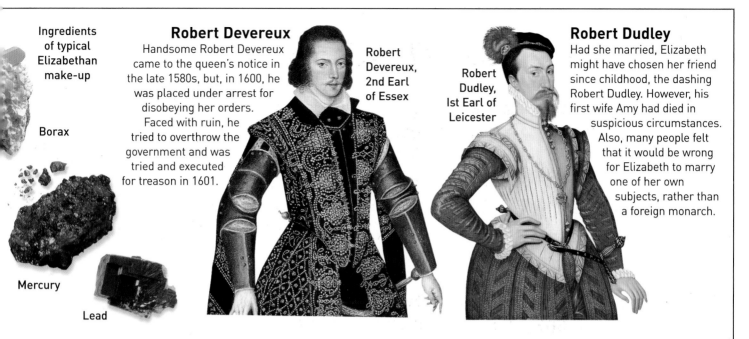

Ingredients of typical Elizabethan make-up

Borax

Mercury

Lead

Robert Devereux

Handsome Robert Devereux came to the queen's notice in the late 1580s, but, in 1600, he was placed under arrest for disobeying her orders. Faced with ruin, he tried to overthrow the government and was tried and executed for treason in 1601.

Robert Devereux, 2nd Earl of Essex

Robert Dudley, 1st Earl of Leicester

Robert Dudley

Had she married, Elizabeth might have chosen her friend since childhood, the dashing Robert Dudley. However, his first wife Amy had died in suspicious circumstances. Also, many people felt that it would be wrong for Elizabeth to marry one of her own subjects, rather than a foreign monarch.

Rallying the troops

Elizabeth was a skilled orator and wrote her own speeches. In 1588, when the Spanish Armada threatened England, she addressed her army at Tilbury, Essex, starting with these famous words: "I know I have the body of a weak and feeble woman, but I have the heart and stomach of a king, and of a king of England too."

Royal gifts

Every New Year, Elizabeth exchanged gifts with her courtiers and servants. She supposedly gave these mittens to Margaret Edgecumbe, a maid of honour, in about 1600.

Carved, gilded mahogany

Silk embroidery with patterns of foliage, a popular 16th-century design

A female skill

This mahogany chair, one of a pair, is said to have been embroidered by the Queen and given to Elizabeth More, one of her ladies-in-waiting. The Queen was an expert needleworker, a lifelong skill she learned as a child.

Ornate low chair

Trade and exploration

In 1497, John Cabot sailed to North America on behalf of Henry VII, and laid the foundations of England's empire there. As the Spanish and Portuguese took over trade across the Atlantic and around the African coast, English seamen searched in vain for new routes to Asia. Piracy was more lucrative, and raiding Spanish treasure ships brought great wealth into England.

How far west?

Sailors had a compass to indicate direction and an astrolabe (above) to gauge the Sun's height at noon to see how far north or south they were – but, crucially, not how far east or west they were.

Crew keep watch for land from crow's-nest

Drake's ships raiding Santo Domingo in the Caribbean

Raiding the Spanish

In 1577–81, Francis Drake became the first Englishman to circumnavigate the globe. On that voyage, he raided several Spanish settlements and came home a rich man. Later, backed by Elizabeth I, he raided more Spanish settlements and ships laden with treasure in the Caribbean.

Looking for China

Italian navigator John Cabot (Giovanni Caboto) believed the quickest route to China was across the North Atlantic. In 1497, he sailed from Bristol with the support of Henry VII, and discovered Newfoundland instead, which he claimed for England.

Walter Raleigh

Adventurer, writer, and courtier, Walter Raleigh established England's first colonies in North America in 1585 and 1587. They were later abandoned but they paved the way for the start of Britain's vast empire.

Silk

Pineapple

Potatoes

Tobacco

Drawing of a native of Virginia by John White, 1585

Luxury goods

The discovery of sea routes to the East Indies, by Spanish and Portuguese traders, meant that silks and spices could be brought back more cheaply than by land. New goods came too – pineapples, tomatoes, and, later, potatoes and tobacco from the Americas.

Cinnamon

Cloves

Peppercorns

New world

The English colonist and artist John White drew everything of interest or importance on his trips to America. This included turtles, pineapples, and the native people, for study and reportage rather than art.

East India Company House, London

Going east

In 1600, Elizabeth I granted a licence to a group of London merchants to challenge the Dutch and Portuguese monopoly of the spice trade in eastern Asia. The East India Company came under attack from the Dutch in Indonesia, but later became highly successful in India.

A replica of Cabot's ship, the *Matthew*

Queen of Scots

In 1567, Mary Queen of Scots was forced to abdicate as a result of her scandalous personal life, and she fled for safety to England. Catholic Mary posed a real threat to her cousin Queen Elizabeth, as some wanted to see her on the English throne. She was held captive for 20 years, and was finally tried for treason and executed.

A French childhood

In 1548, five-year-old Mary was sent to France. She may have lived at Chenonceau. In 1558, she married the heir, or dauphin, to the French throne. In 1560, Mary was widowed, aged just 18. She returned to Scotland, almost a stranger in her own land.

Francis, the dauphin of France

Royal scandal

By the age of 25, Mary had been married three times and widowed twice. Mary's third husband, the Earl of Bothwell, had been divorced just 12 days when he married her, and was suspected of murdering her second husband. Her subjects forced her to abdicate.

Mary dancing with Lord Darnley

Lord Darnley

Mary's second husband was her cousin, Lord Darnley. Their son became James VI of Scotland and, after the death of Elizabeth, King of England. Insanely jealous of Mary's secretary, David Rizzio, Darnley stabbed him to death in front of Mary. Months later, he himself was murdered.

Baby queen

Mary was born in 1542 in the royal palace of Linlithgow. Six days later her father, James V, died. Crowned Queen of Scotland at nine months, Mary lost the title in 1567.

Catholic threat

Mary sought refuge in England but was a threat to the throne. Many Catholics saw Elizabeth as the illegitimate daughter of Henry VIII and his mistress, Anne Boleyn. Mary, a legitimate descendant of Henry VIII's older sister Margaret, was seen as his true heir.

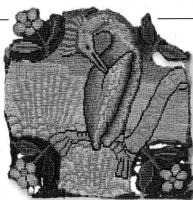

Stitching time

Mary spent 20 years in prison in England. She filled her days with reading, letter writing, and doing embroidery. A detail from her beautiful Oxburgh Hanging is shown here.

Mary's own prayer book and rosary beads

Royal spymaster

Principal royal secretary Sir Francis Walsingham ran a network of agents to spy on Elizabeth's enemies. In 1586, he infiltrated a plot by the Catholic Anthony Babington to assassinate Elizabeth. Mary was implicated in the plot and put on trial for treason.

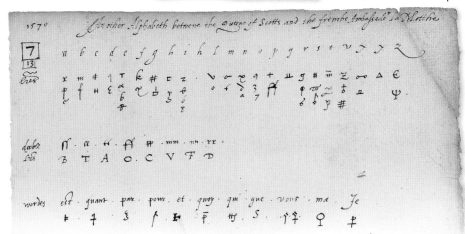

Secret code

While in prison, Mary wrote letters in code, using 23 symbols for letters of the alphabet and 36 more for whole words. However, all her letters were intercepted and decoded, and codebreaker Thomas Phelippes set a trap to identify her co-conspirators.

Warrant to Execute Mary Stuart

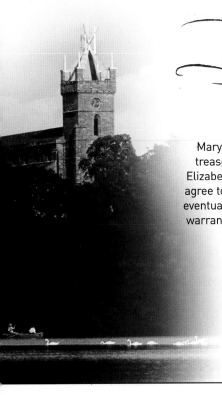

Death warrant

Mary was found guilty of treason in October 1586. Elizabeth was reluctant to agree to her execution, but eventually signed the death warrant on 1 February 1587.

The execution

Mary was beheaded at Fotheringhay Castle on 8 February 1587. Her death shocked her son, by now James VI of Scotland, and appalled Catholic Europe. It also helped Phillip II of Spain to justify the Armada he was about to launch against England.

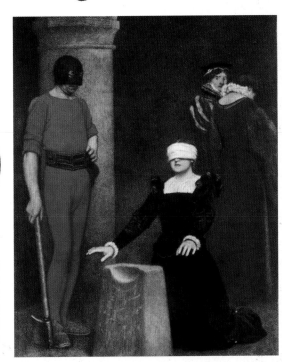

The Armada

In 1588, Spain launched a huge fleet, the Armada, to invade England. Outraged by England's support of Dutch rebels fighting for independence from Spain, and by the execution of the Catholic Mary Queen of Scots, Philip II of Spain was determined to overthrow Elizabeth. But he was foiled by English seamanship, artillery, and bad weather.

Playing for time
In April 1587, Sir Francis Drake set back Spain's invasion plans when he raided their fleet at anchor in Cadiz, Spain, destroying 37 ships. This gave the English vital time to prepare.

Wheel-mounted cannon

Battle tactics
The Spanish and English fleets deployed their cannons in different ways. The Spanish used guns at close range to stop an enemy ship before coming alongside and boarding it. The English mounted theirs on four-wheeled gun-carriages, so they could easily fire, pull back, reload, and fire again to damage or even sink the ship.

Cannon balls

The Armada, 1590s, English school

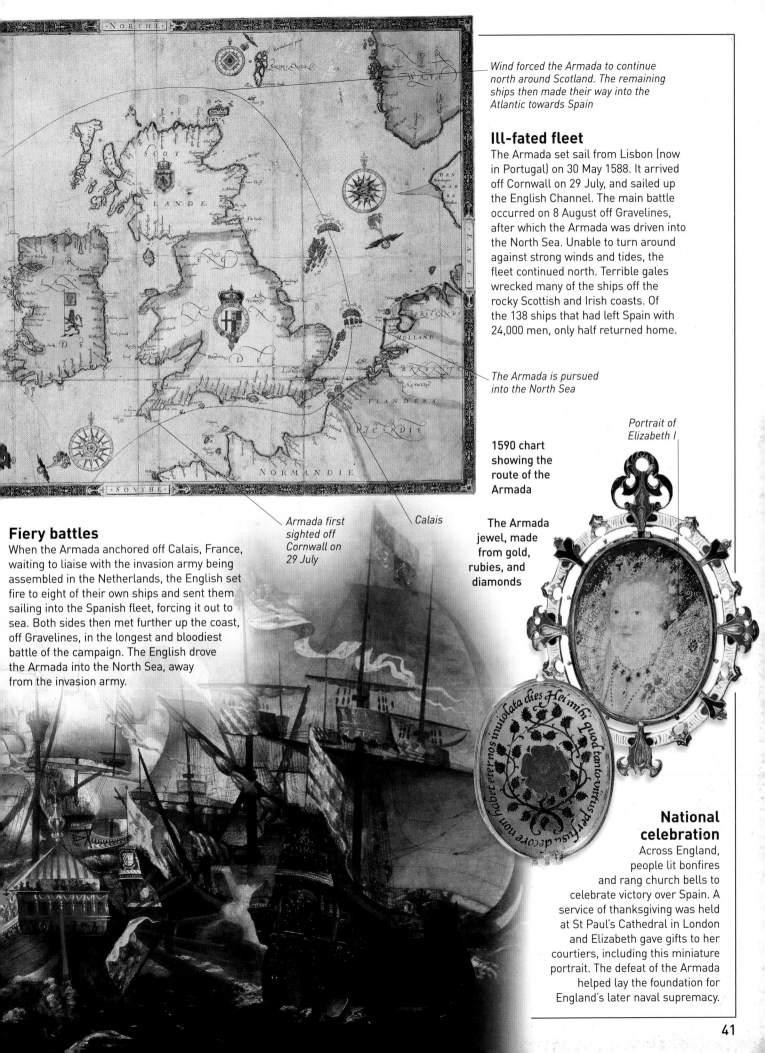

Wind forced the Armada to continue north around Scotland. The remaining ships then made their way into the Atlantic towards Spain

Ill-fated fleet

The Armada set sail from Lisbon (now in Portugal) on 30 May 1588. It arrived off Cornwall on 29 July, and sailed up the English Channel. The main battle occurred on 8 August off Gravelines, after which the Armada was driven into the North Sea. Unable to turn around against strong winds and tides, the fleet continued north. Terrible gales wrecked many of the ships off the rocky Scottish and Irish coasts. Of the 138 ships that had left Spain with 24,000 men, only half returned home.

The Armada is pursued into the North Sea

1590 chart showing the route of the Armada

Portrait of Elizabeth I

The Armada jewel, made from gold, rubies, and diamonds

Armada first sighted off Cornwall on 29 July

Calais

Fiery battles

When the Armada anchored off Calais, France, waiting to liaise with the invasion army being assembled in the Netherlands, the English set fire to eight of their own ships and sent them sailing into the Spanish fleet, forcing it out to sea. Both sides then met further up the coast, off Gravelines, in the longest and bloodiest battle of the campaign. The English drove the Armada into the North Sea, away from the invasion army.

National celebration

Across England, people lit bonfires and rang church bells to celebrate victory over Spain. A service of thanksgiving was held at St Paul's Cathedral in London and Elizabeth gave gifts to her courtiers, including this miniature portrait. The defeat of the Armada helped lay the foundation for England's later naval supremacy.

Tudor London

Street sellers

At the heart of Tudor England was the capital city, London, by far the biggest city in the country and one of the largest in Europe. Between 1500 and 1600, the population grew from 50,000 to about 200,000. Spread across the River Thames, the bustling city was the centre of England's government, trade, and commerce.

St Paul's cathedral

Globe Theatre

View of London from the south by Claes Jans Visscher, c.1616

Waterman

London Bridge, where traitors' heads were displayed on poles

London's layout
The historic centre of the city was enclosed by 4 km (2½ miles) of walls, first built by the Romans. But London had already spread beyond these city walls. The palace of Whitehall and Westminster, home of parliament, lay to its west, and south of the River Thames was Southwark, across London Bridge.

Tower of London
On the north bank of the Thames, the Tower of London guarded the city. Henry VII and his son had royal quarters there, but its main use during Tudor times was as a state prison.

Lanterns, as used by Tudor nightwatchmen

Curfew at dusk
Every evening at dusk, the city gates were closed, shops and taverns shut, and everyone went home. After dark, streets were patrolled by nightwatchmen to deter criminals.

Waterborne
As London Bridge was the city's only river crossing, watermen operated more than 2,000 wherries – long, light rowing boats – to take passengers up and down the river or across to the other bank.

Running London
The Lord Mayor was elected to govern the city and administer justice. The everyday work in running London was carried out by the Court of Common Council.

Tudor food to go
Fresh fish, fruit and vegetables, sausages and other meats, hot pies, baked apples, and a wide range of pastries could all be bought from street sellers, whose distinctive cries advertised their wares.

Tudor shopping
Traders or craftsmen selling similar goods often formed guilds, such as the Baker's Guild, and had shops on the same street. Tailors, for instance, could be found in Threadneedle Street, and shoemakers in Shoe Lane.

Upper stories jut out into the street to increase space inside the house

Street life
London's many pickpockets, or cutpurses, used a knife to cut the strings that tied a purse to its owner's belt. Some were trained at an illegal "school" near Billingsgate Market.

Tudor buildings
Within the bustling warren of narrow, winding streets, London's houses and shops were mostly built of clay brick or wood, as both were readily available locally. A few were constructed of stone removed from the recently closed monasteries and friaries.

Tudor entertainment

The rich jousted, played chess, and put on short plays with music, called masques. Bowls, tennis, and archery were popular, as were hunting and hawking in fine weather. The poor had more unruly pursuits. Football teams of unlimited size kicked or threw the ball through fields or city streets. All classes enjoyed animal baiting and, by the end of the period, the theatre.

Musical times

Music was a common form of entertainment – from the bagpipes and the shawm (a simple woodwind instrument) of the poor to the lute or the virginals (a keyboard instrument) of the rich. Folk songs and ballads were also popular.

Bagpipes

Lute

Sheep-gut strings, plucked with fingers and thumb

Children enjoying a game of chess

Games of skill

Chess and other board games were popular in the Tudor age. Chess is the oldest game of skill in the world, dating back to before 600 CE in Asia. New rules were introduced to make the game more exciting, and these are still in place today.

Horse wore special robes decorated with rider's heraldic coat of arms

Jousting for honour

The greatest sport for nobles was the tournament. Originally a medieval training exercise for war, by the Tudor age the event was more about chivalry and show. The highlight was the joust, where knights on horseback charged towards one another and tried to unseat each other with a lance.

Protective headgear

Brittle wooden lance designed to shatter on hard impact, minimizing danger

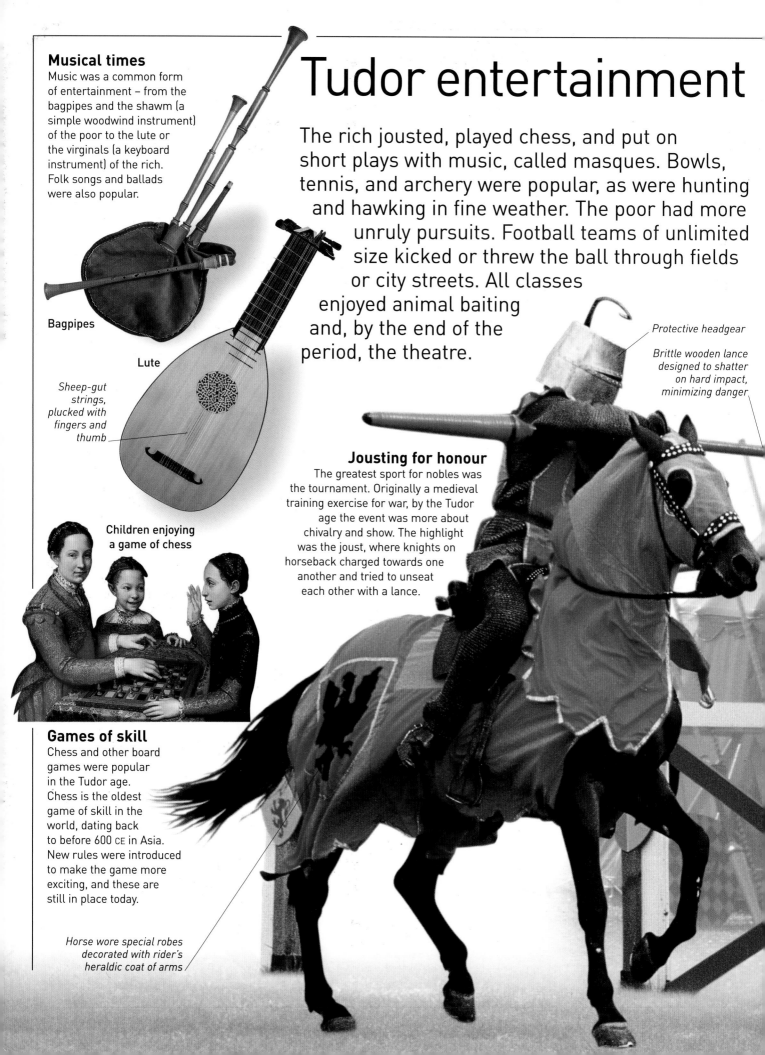

Real tennis

The original indoor game was so popular with the monarchy that it later became known as real or royal tennis. It was played using leather balls stuffed with human hair. Poor women would sell their hair for the balls as a source of income.

A dog's chance

The cruel sport of bear-baiting was popular with all classes. Monarchs and nobles kept their own bears, while poorer people went to public bear-baits. The bear was tied to a post and attacked by dogs.

The theatre

Travelling players performed plays in the street, as theatres were found only in London. At the start of the Tudor era, morality plays dealt with human vice and religious virtue. By the end, Shakespeare (p. 47) and Christopher Marlowe were writing plays that are still performed today.

A performance of Shakespeare's *Hamlet*

Cocks fighting, using their beaks and feet

Heraldic coat of arms

Cockfighting

Watching a pair of cockerels fight each other to the death was common entertainment. At the cockpit near Smithfield in London, spectators paid one penny to watch the contest.

Competitors separated by wooden rail

End of an era

The death of the childless Elizabeth I in 1603 marked the end of the Tudor dynasty. The new king of England was James I, a member of the Stuart family, which had ruled Scotland since 1371. His reign brought England and Scotland under one ruler for the first time. Although the Tudor period was relatively short, it left behind much of value.

Elizabeth I's funeral procession

Death of a queen
Elizabeth's death was widely mourned. One thousand people walked in her funeral procession and tens of thousands turned out to see her final journey from Whitehall Palace to Westminster Abbey, where she was buried in Henry VII's chapel.

The British Empire
The Tudor era saw Newfoundland become Britain's first overseas possession in 1583, and initial colonies set up by Sir Walter Raleigh paved the way for later, more successful ones on the east coast of America. The East India Company, set up in 1600, began to build up the trading networks that would lead to the growth of the largest empire in history.

Designs for the union flag

Union flag
On the succession of James I, designs were drawn up to represent the union of England and Scotland. The new flag, first flown in 1606 and a forerunner of today's union flag, placed the English and Scottish flags on top of one another.

The King
The crown passed to the son of Mary Queen of Scots, James VI of Scotland, who then also became James I of England. He had been King of Scotland for 36 years, since the age of one. His accession to the English throne marks the start of the Stuart dynasty.

Ornate architecture
A new style of architecture emerged in the Tudor period. Buildings were constructed from darkened wood beams. White-washed plaster was then used to fill in the structure to give a contrast to the dark timber and create striking patterns, as shown here at Little Moreton Hall, in Cheshire.

Poster for the 1966 film about Henry VIII, *A Man for all Seasons*

Poster for the 1998 film *Elizabeth*

Universal artist
The greatest artistic legacy of the Tudor age is William Shakespeare's plays. Although 13 of his 37 plays were written after Elizabeth I's death, he is considered an Elizabethan playwright. His plays have never gone out of fashion and are still performed all over the world.

William Shakespeare (1564–1616)

The Tudors today
Many of the Tudor period's main events and characters – Henry VIII and his six wives, the reign of Elizabeth I, Mary Queen of Scots' tragic life – have been kept alive through films, plays, and novels, as well as history books.

A performance of Shakespeare's comedy *A Midsummer Night's Dream* in 2001

Index

AB

Anne of Cleves 21
apprentices 26, 27
aristocracy 10, 11
Armada 35, 39, 40–41
armour 18–19
Arthur, Prince 6, 20
Askew, Anne 23
Babington, Anthony 39
bear-baiting 45
beggars 17
Bible 23, 26
Boleyn, Anne 20, 21, 30, 32, 39
Books of Hours 20, 23
Bosworth Field, Battle of 6, 7
Bothwell, Earl of 38
bows 19
British Empire 46

C

Cabot, John 36
Calais 29, 41
Cambridge University 27
cannons 18, 40
Caribbean 9, 36
Catherine of Aragon 15, 20, 33
Catholic Church 17, 19, 22, 24, 25, 28–29, 30, 39
Caxton, William 9
Cecil, William 31
Chaucer, Geoffrey 9
chess 44
children 16, 23, 26–27, 44
China 36
Church of England 22–23, 24, 31
churches 25, 31
cities 42–43
clothes 10, 11, 27, 32–33
cockfighting 45
colonies 37, 46
Columbus, Christopher 9
Coverdale, Miles 23
craftsmen 10, 43
Cranmer, Thomas 24, 29
crime 16, 17, 42, 43
Cromwell, Thomas 23
curfew 42

DE

Darnley, Lord 38
Deal 19
death 16, 17
defence 18–19
Deptford 18
Devereux, Robert 35
diseases 16, 34
dissolution 22, 23
doctors 16
Drake, Sir Francis 36, 40
East India Company 37, 46
education 23, 26
Edward V King, 8
Edward VI, King 6, 20, 24, 25, 26, 28
Elizabeth I, Queen 6, 28, 30–31, 47
birth 20
clothes 33
death 8, 46
"golden age" 34–35
and Mary Queen of Scots 38, 39
trade and exploration 36, 37
Elizabeth of York 7, 8
entertainment 27, 44–45
Erasmus, Desiderius 14, 26
executions 17, 20, 21, 39
exploration 9, 36–37

FG

farming 10
feasts 11, 12–13
Field of the Cloth-of-old, 15
firearms 18, 19
Fisher, John 9
flags 18, 19
Flodden, Battle of 18
food 12–13, 43
football 27, 44
forts 18, 19
Fountains Abbey 22
Foxe, John 29
France 15, 19, 29, 38, 41
Francis I, King of France 15
Francis II, King of France 38
furniture 35
Gardiner, Stephen 29
glasses 12
Gravelines, Battle of 41
Greenwich 19, 20
Grey, Lady Jane 7, 28

HI

Hardwick Hall 11
Hatfield House 30
Hell 17
Henry VII, King 6, 7, 8–9, 14, 36, 42
Henry VIII, King 6, 7, 24, 47
banquets 12
breaks with Rome 22–23
court 14–15
navy 18, 19
successor 20, 24, 39
wives 20–21
hawking 15
herbs 12, 16
Holbein, Hans 14, 15
Holy Roman Empire 19
horses 44–45
hospitals 25
houses 10, 11, 43, 47
Howard, Catherine 20, 21
hunting 15
India 37
Ireland 41

JKL

James I, King 7, 38, 39, 46
James IV, King of Scotland 18
James V, King of Scotland 7, 18, 38
jewellery 27, 30, 32, 34
John of Gaunt 6
jousting 15, 44–45
kitchens 12
knives 12
Lancaster, house of 6–7, 8
laws 32
Leicester, Robert Dudley, 1st Earl of 35
life expectancy 16
Little Moreton Hall 47
London 10, 16, 42–43, 45
London Bridge 17, 42
Lord Mayor 43
Luther, Martin 22

MNO

make-up 33, 34
manuscripts 20, 23
Margaret Tudor 7
market towns 10
Marlowe, Christopher 45
marriage 26
Mary, Virgin 25
Mary I, Queen 6, 20, 28, 30, 38
Mary Queen of Scots 7, 38–39, 40, 46, 47
Mary Rose 18
marzipan (marchpane) 13
masks 16
meat 13
medicine 16
merchants 14, 42
middle class 10, 11
monasteries 22–23
music 14, 30, 44
navigation 36
navy 18, 19, 40–41
Netherlands 37, 41
Newfoundland 36, 46
nightwatchmen 42
nobility 10, 11, 32, 44
North America 36, 37, 46
Northumberland, John Dudley, Duke of 24
Oxford University, 27

P

paintings 34
Parker, Matthew 31
Parr, Catherine 21, 23
Pembroke Castle 6
Phelippes, Thomas 39
Philip II, King of Spain 29, 39, 40
pickpockets 43
pirates 36
pistols 19
plague 16
plays 44, 45, 47
pomanders 16
Pope 22, 24
Portugal 36, 37
Protestant Church 17, 23, 24–25, 28, 29, 30, 31
punishments 16, 17, 26

R

Raleigh, Sir Walter 37, 46
Reformation 22, 24–25
religion 22–25, 28, 31
Renaissance 8, 14
Richard III, King 6
Richmond Palace 8
Rizzio, David 38
rosaries 25, 39
Royal Grammar School, Guildford 26

S

St Mary Bethlehem hospital 25
St Paul's Cathedral 41
Santo Domingo 36
schools 26
Scotland 18, 38, 41, 46
Seymour, Jane 20
Shakespeare, William 45, 46, 47
ships 9, 18, 19, 36–37, 40–41
shoes 33
shops 43
Simnel, Lambert 8
smallpox 34
soldiers 6, 18, 19
Somerset, Edward Seymour, Duke of, 24
Southwark 42
Spain 29, 36, 37, 40–41
spices 12, 13, 37
spoons 12

TUV

tennis 44, 45
Thames, River 18, 42
theatres 44, 45, 47
tools 18
Torrigiano, Pietro 8
torture 16, 17, 23, 29
tournaments 15, 44–45
Tower of London 17, 21, 30, 42
towns 10
toys 27
trade 10, 12, 36–37, 42, 43, 46
treason 17, 20, 23, 30, 35, 39
trenchers 13
universities 27
Virginia 37
Visscher, Claes Jans 42

WY

Wales 7
Walsingham, Sir Francis 39
Warbeck, Perkin 8
warfare 18–19
Wars of the Roses 6, 7, 8
weapons 19, 40
weddings 11
Westminster Abbey 9, 31, 46
wherries 42
White, John 37
Whitehall Palace 31, 42, 46
windows 11
Wolsey, Cardinal Thomas 14
wool trade 10
writing 26
Wyatt rebellion 28
yeomen farmers 10
Yeomen of the Guard 8
York, house of 6, 7, 8–9

Stuart family 46

sugar 12, 13
Sumptuary Laws 32, 33
swords 19, 20

Acknowledgements

Dorling Kindersley would like to thank: James Marks & Jody Harding of Hever Castle, Kent; The Knights of Royal England; The Cake Fairy; make-up artist Amanda Wright; Sheila Collins, Joe Conneally, Stefan Podhorodecki, Sarah Pownall & Bradley Round for modelling; and Hilary Bird for the index.

For this relaunch edition, the publisher would also like to thank: Camilla Hallinan for text editing, and Carron Brown for proofreading.

The publisher would like to thank the following for their kind permission to reproduce their photographs:

2 Reproduced by kind permission of His Grace the Duke of Norfolk, Arundel Castle, and of the Baroness Herries: cb; By permission of the Friends of Preston St Mary Church: tc; Hever Castle: cbr; 3 AKG London: tr; Bridgeman Art Library, London/New York: tl; 4 National Maritime Museum, London: reproduced by kind permission of the Chequers Estate cla; Courtesy of the Trustees of the V&A: c; 6 Bridgeman Art Library, London/ New York: Board of Trustees: National Museums & Galleries on Merseyside: br; British Library, London tl; National Portrait Gallery c; Philip Mould, Historical Portraits Ltd, London, UK cra, cr; Topham Picturepoint: cr, cr, bc. 7 Bridgeman Art Library, London/New York: Chelsea Physic Garden, London tc; Phillips, The International Fine Art Auctioneers, UK tl; Roy Miles Fine Paintings clb; The Stapleton Collection c; Victoria & Albert Museum, London, UK cl; Corbis: Jason Hawkes br; Dean and Chapter of York: reproduced by kind permission tr; 8 V & A, Bridgeman Art Library, London/New York: cra, clb, cal; 8–9 Topham Picturepoint: bc; 9 AKG London: br; Ancient Art &

Architecture Collection: cr; Bridgeman Art Library, London/New York: tr, clb; DK Images: British Library cra; Topham Picturepoint: cbl; 10 Bridgeman Art Library, London/New York: cal; DK Images: Museum of English Rural Life cl; Museum of London cbl; 11 Bridgeman Art Library, London/New York: Hatfield House, Hertfordshire tr; Corbis: Eric Crighton c; 12 Hever Castle: bc; Historic Royal Palaces Enterprises: Crown copyright: Historic Royal Palaces tl; Courtesy of the Trustees of the V&A: cb, bl, cbl. 13 Bridgeman Art Library, London/New York: Ashmolean Museum br; Courtesy of the Trustees of the V&A: bcl; 14 AKG London: British Library br; Bridgeman Art Library, London/New York: tl, cl, cr; Lebrecht Collection: bl; 15 AKG London: br; Bridgeman Art Library, London/New York: cl; The College of Arms: cra; 16 Bridgeman Art Library, London/New York: tcl; Asprey & Co bcl; DK Images: Science Museum tl; 16–17 Hever Castle; 17 Bridgeman Art Library, London/New York: tcr; Bibliotheque Saint Genevieve, Paris crb; Corbis: by kind permission of the Trustees of the National Gallery, London bc; Mary Evans Picture Library: tr; Hever Castle: tc, cra; 18 Bridgeman Art Library, London/New York: Musee d'Orsay, Paris cla; DK Images: National Maritime Museum bl, bc; Mary Evans Picture Library: tl, cb; 19 Bridgeman Art Library, London/New York: bc; DK Images: Wallace Collection cr; Warwick Castle cra; Topham Picturepoint: tr; Warwick Castle: c; 20 Bridgeman Art Library, London/ New York: National Gallery of Art, Washington DC, USA tl; Hever Castle: tc, bl; Topham Picturepoint: cr, cb, bcl; 20–21 Bridgeman Art Library, London/New York: Mark Fiennes / Sudeley Castle, Winchcombe, Gloucestershire, UK; 21 Bridgeman Art Library, London/New York: The Stapleton Collection ca; Corbis: Jean Pierre Lescourret br; Hever Castle: tr; Topham Picturepoint: tr, cla; 22

AKG London: c; Corbis: Archivo Iconografico cla; Gianni Dagli Orti tl; Rex Features: bc; 23 Bridgeman Art Library, London/ New York: Archives Charmet/ Bibliotheque Mazarine, Paris, France cra; The Stapleton Collection bc; DK Images: British Library cl; Topham Picturepoint: tc; 24–25 Bridgeman Art Library, London/ New York: National Portrait Gallery, London, UK; The Stapleton Collection tr; The Trustees of the Weston Park Foundation tl; 25 Bridgeman Art Library, London/New York: Guildhall Library, Corporation of London, UK tc; Corbis: Adam Woolfitt cl; Glasgow Museum cbl; Museum of Order of St. John b; Sonia Halliday Photographs: F.H.C. Birch crb; 26 AKG London: clb; 27 Bridgeman Art Library, London/ New York: Kunsthistorisches Museum, Vienna, Austria c, crb; The Berger Collection at Denver Art Museum, USA bc; Corbis: Hulton–Deutch Collection cla; Museum Of London: cra; 28 Bridgeman Art Library, London/New York: National Portrait Gallery, London, UK bl; Mary Evans Picture Library: tr; 29 Bridgeman Art Library, London/New York: tr, bcl; Christie's Images, London, UK cl; Giraudon/ Louvre, Paris, France cr; British Library: t ; 30 Ancient Art & Architecture Collection: M&J Lynch cr; Bridgeman Art Library, London/New York: tl; Hamberg Kunsthalle, Hamburg, Germany cb; Mark Fiennes/ Helmingham Hall, Suffolk, UK bc; National Maritime Museum, London: reproduced by kind permission of the Chequers Estate cla, c; 31 Bridgeman Art Library, London/New York: Burghley House Collection, Lincolnshire, UK cra; Lambeth Palace, London, UK c; The College of Arms: t; By permission of the Friends of Preston St Mary Church: crb; Tophoto : bc; 32 Museum Of London: cl; 34 The British Museum: MI 116–48 clb; DK Images: Natural History Museum tl; Courtesy of the Trustees of the V&A: tc, bl; St Faith's Church, Gaywood, Norfolk, UK c; Yale Center for British Art, Paul Mellon Collection, USA tcr; DK Images: Natural History Museum cla; Courtesy of the Trustees of the V&A: cb; 36 DK Images: National Maritime Museum cl; 36–37 Getty Images: Clive Mason c; 37 Bridgeman Art Library, London/New York: Ashmolean

Museum bcr; National Portrait Gallery of Ireland, Dublin tl; DK Images: British Museum tr, Charlestown Shipwreck & Heritage Centre c; Museum Of London: cla; Topham Picturepoint: British Museum c; 38 AKG London: Victoria and Albert Museum bl; Bridgeman Art Library, London/New York: cl; Corbis: Michael Nicholson cal; Sandro Xannini br; Wolfgang Kaehler tl. 39 Reproduced by kind permission of His Grace the Duke of Norfolk, Arundel Castle, and of the Baroness Herries: tl; Bridgeman Art Library, London /New York: cl; Mary Evans Picture Library: br; Public Record Office: cra; Tophoto : cb; Courtesy of the Trustees of the V&A Picture Library: tcr; 40 DK Images: Mary Rose Trust cl; National Maritime Museum c; 40–41 Bridgeman Art Library, London/ New York: Society of Apothecaries bc; National Portrait Gallery, London, UK tl; National Maritime Museum c; 41 Courtesy of the Trustees of the V&A: Mr D.P. Naish cr; 42 Bridgeman Art Library, London/New York: British Library crb. 42 British Library: ca. 42 Mary Evans Picture Library: tc, clb, tcl, tcr. 43 The Bridgeman Art Library: The Stapleton Collection tc; 43 Bridgeman Art Library, London/New York: British Library tcl; DK Images: Weald and Downland Open Air Museum cr; 44 AKG London: clb; 44–45 Knights of Royal England: bc; 45 Bridgeman Art Library, London/New York: c; 46 Corbis: Gianni Dagli Orti bc; DK Images: National Maritime Museum tl; National Library Of Scotland: The Trustees of the National Library of Scotland cr; 46–47 British Library; 47 Corbis: Bettmann c; Robbie Jack bc; Robert Estall tr; 47 Moviestore Collection: cl; Rex Features: Everett cal.

Wallchart: The Bridgeman Art Library: National Portrait Gallery, London fcl; Richard Philp, London fcl; Walker Art Gallery, National Museums, Liverpool c; Woburn Abbey, Bedfordshire bl; Crown copyright: Historic Royal Palaces: crb; DK Images: British Museum tl (coin); English Heritage clb; Stephen Oliver cla; Sister Susanna fclb; Getty Images: The Bridgeman Art Library / Nicholas Hilliard tl (Elizabeth I)

All other images: © Dorling Kindersley
For further information see www.dkimages.com